CHRISTMAS
Activity Book for Kids

Mazes, Coloring and Puzzles for kids Ages 4 - 8

Young Scholar

Young Scholar
Published by Ciparum LLC

Christmas Activity Book for Kids

ISBN-10:1-945601-32-9
ISBN-13:978-1-945601-32-3

My Name

Match the shadow to the right Santa.

HELP SANTA CATCH UP WITH RUDOLPH

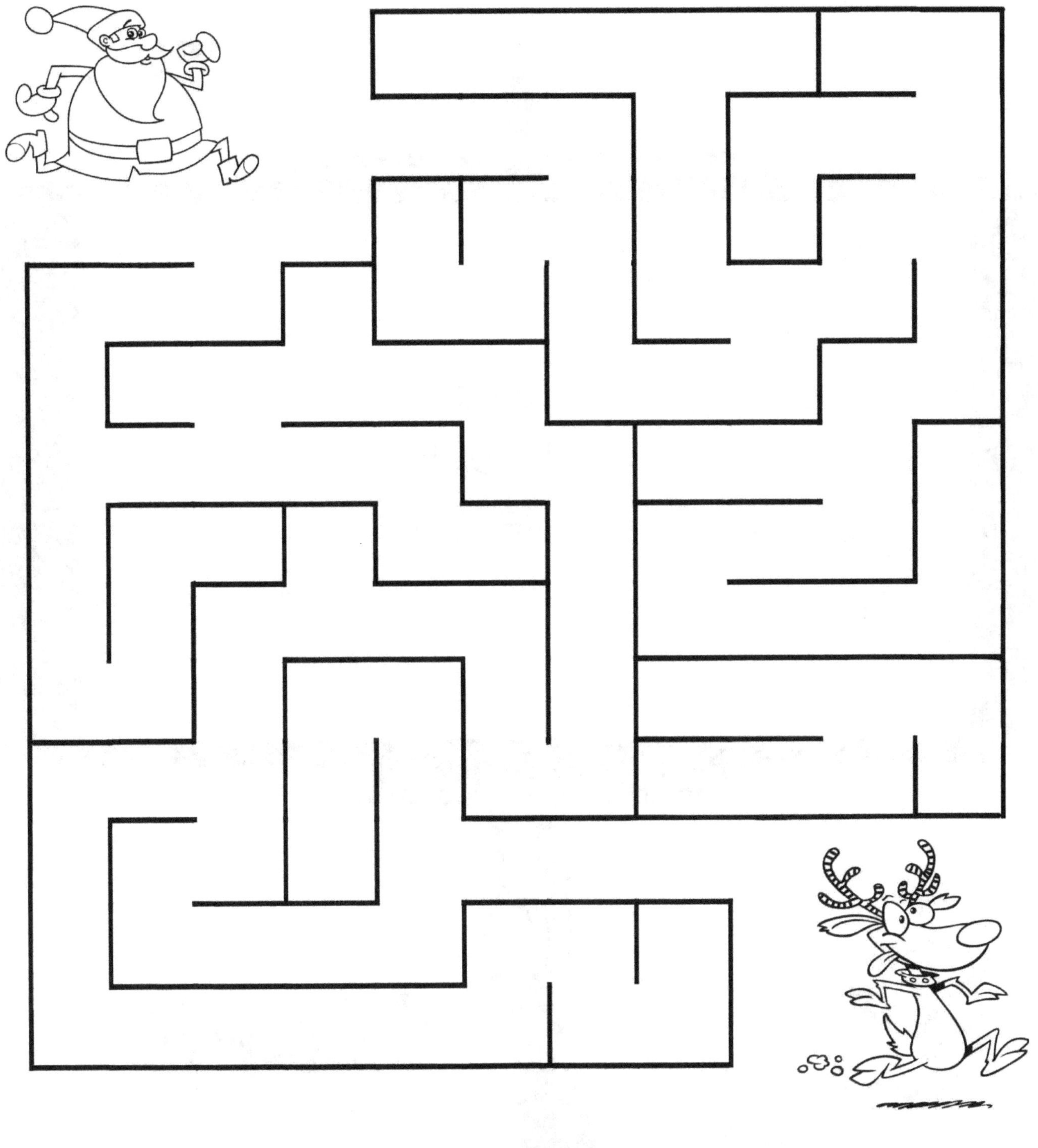

SANTA & ____________

write your name here

SELFIE

WHAT I WANT FOR CHRISTMAS
Define Naughty!
Define Nice!
DEAR SANTA,
cut & mail to Santa

FUN!

FIND 5 DIFFERENCES

Answer on next page

FUN!

FIND 5 DIFFERENCES

COLOR ME!

dot to dot

connect the dots and color!

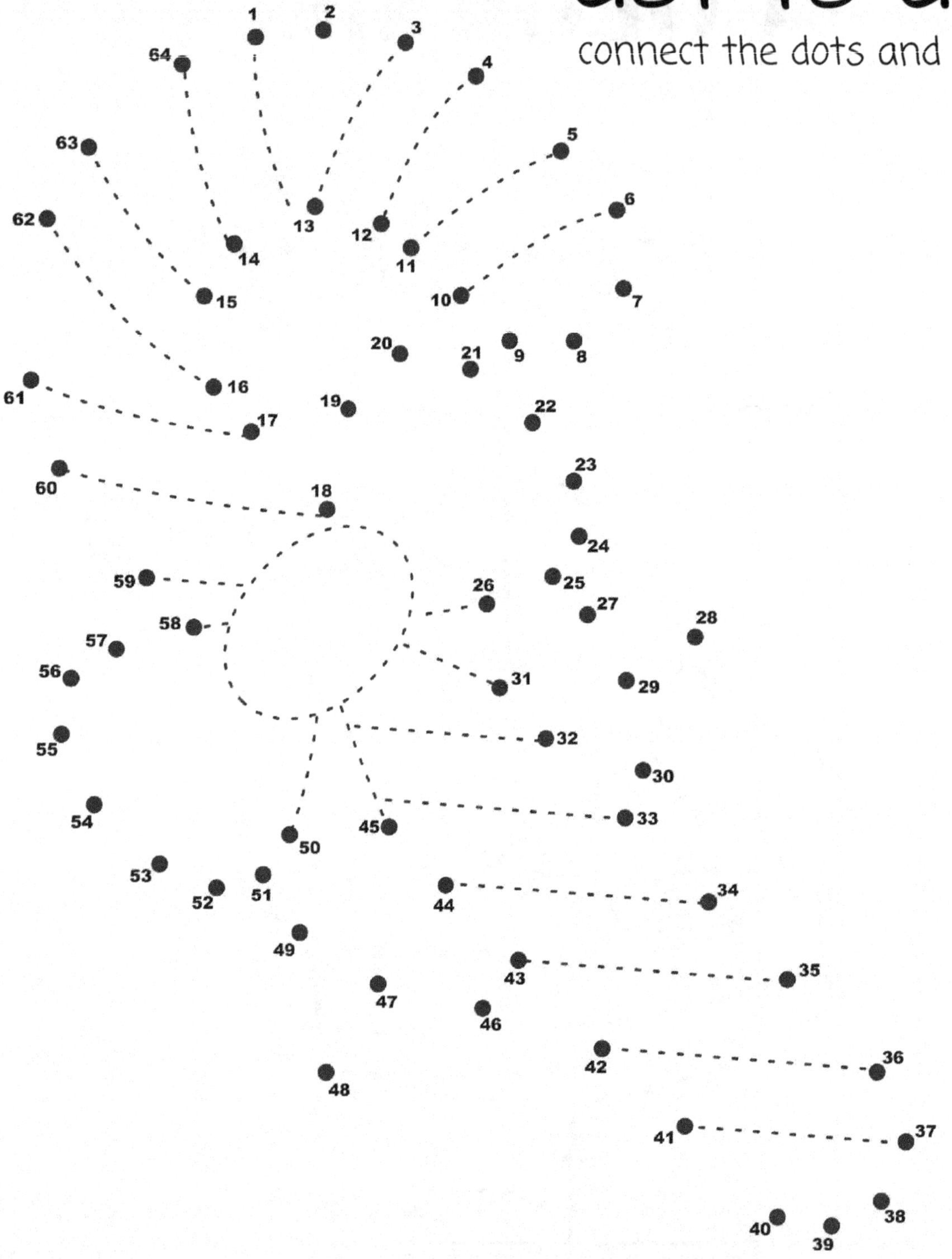

Sharpen your mind!

1. Mitten 2. Present 3. Bell 4. Star
5. (across) Snowflake 5. (down) Santa
6. Fireplace 7. Cookie 8. Snowman
9. Tree 10. Hat 11. Ball 12. Candle

Santa
North Pole

COLOR & CUT!

Color the image and carefully cut using a scissors
Make a hole, add a string and hang on the Christmas tree.

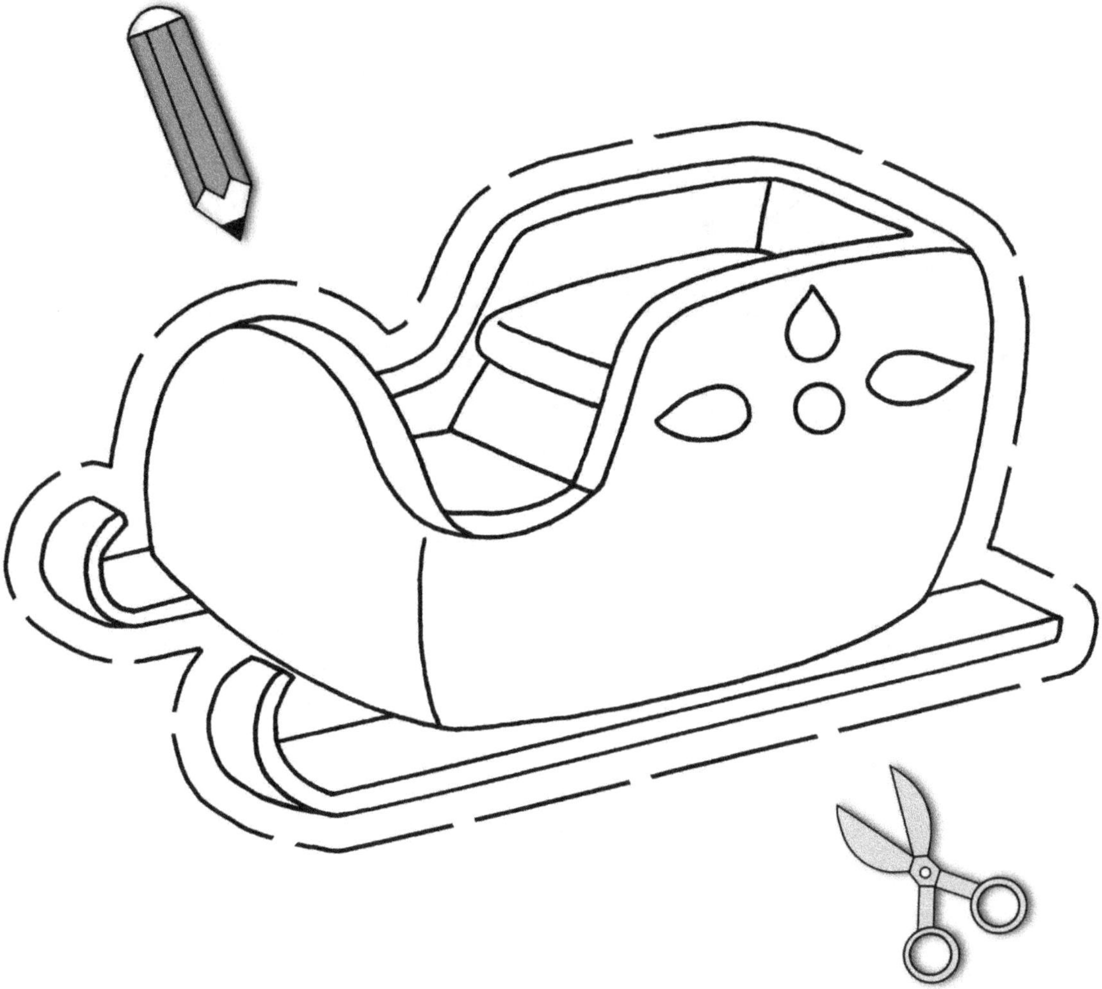

Color Me!

Path finder

HELP MARY FIND HER PRESENT

grid draw

Use the grid as a guide and draw the image

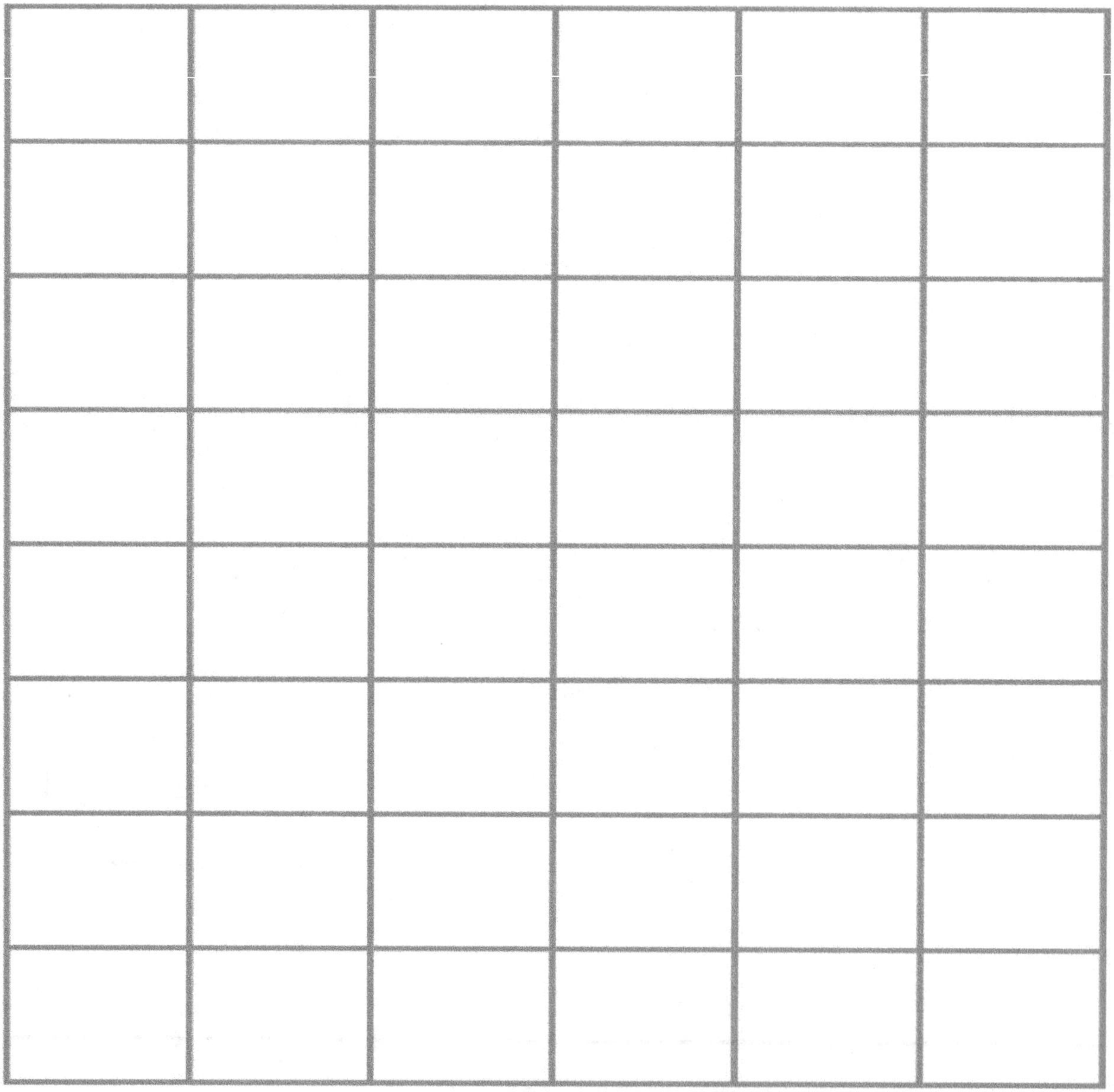

HOW MANY SANTAS DO YOU SEE?

ANSWER ON THE NEXT PAGE

HOW MANY SANTAS DO YOU SEE?

?

ANSWER 17

COLOR 2 SIMILAR MUGS

dot to dot

Connect and color

Complete and Color

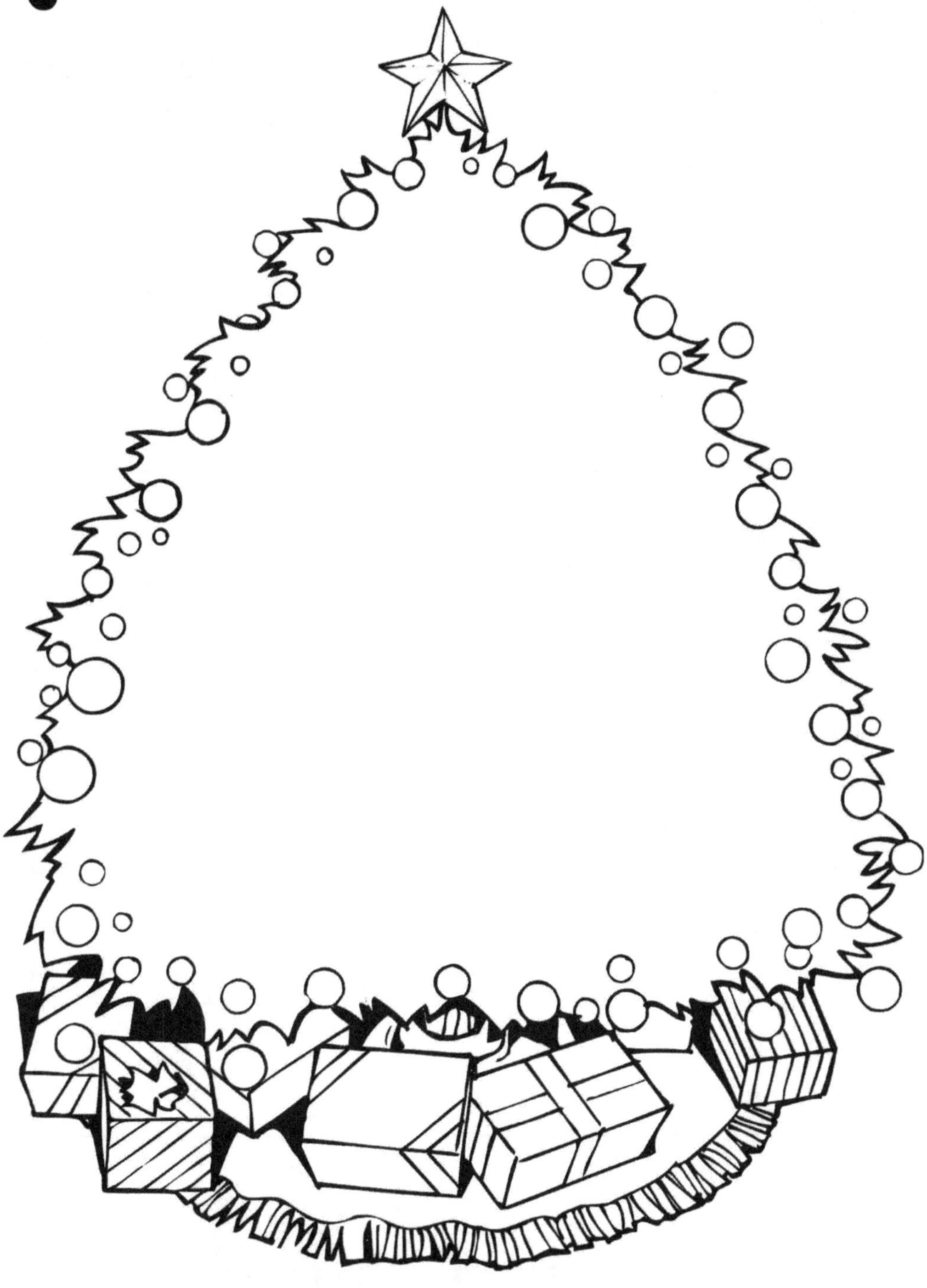

Grid Drawing

Use the grid as a guide.
Draw the image

HELP THE ELF

COLOR & CUT!

Color the image and carefully cut using a scissors
Make a hole, add a string and hang on the Christmas tree.

How many snowmen do you see?

Who am I?

Frosty Rudolph

Alabaster Santa

HELP THE ELF

unscramble the words
1. lenga ....
2.urasovi ....
3.ussej ....
4.ramgen ....
Answer on next page

Help the Elf

unscramble the words
1. lenga angel
2.urasovi saviour
3.ussej Jesus
4.ramgen manger

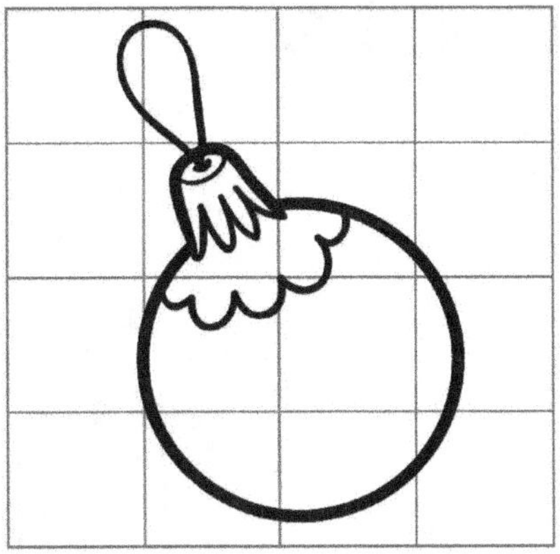

grid draw

Use the grid as a guide.
Draw the image

Which Alphabet marks Toms present?

Match each Santa to his shadow

COLOR & CUT

Color the image. Carefully cut with a scissors.
Make a hole and run a string through. Hang on the Christmas tree.

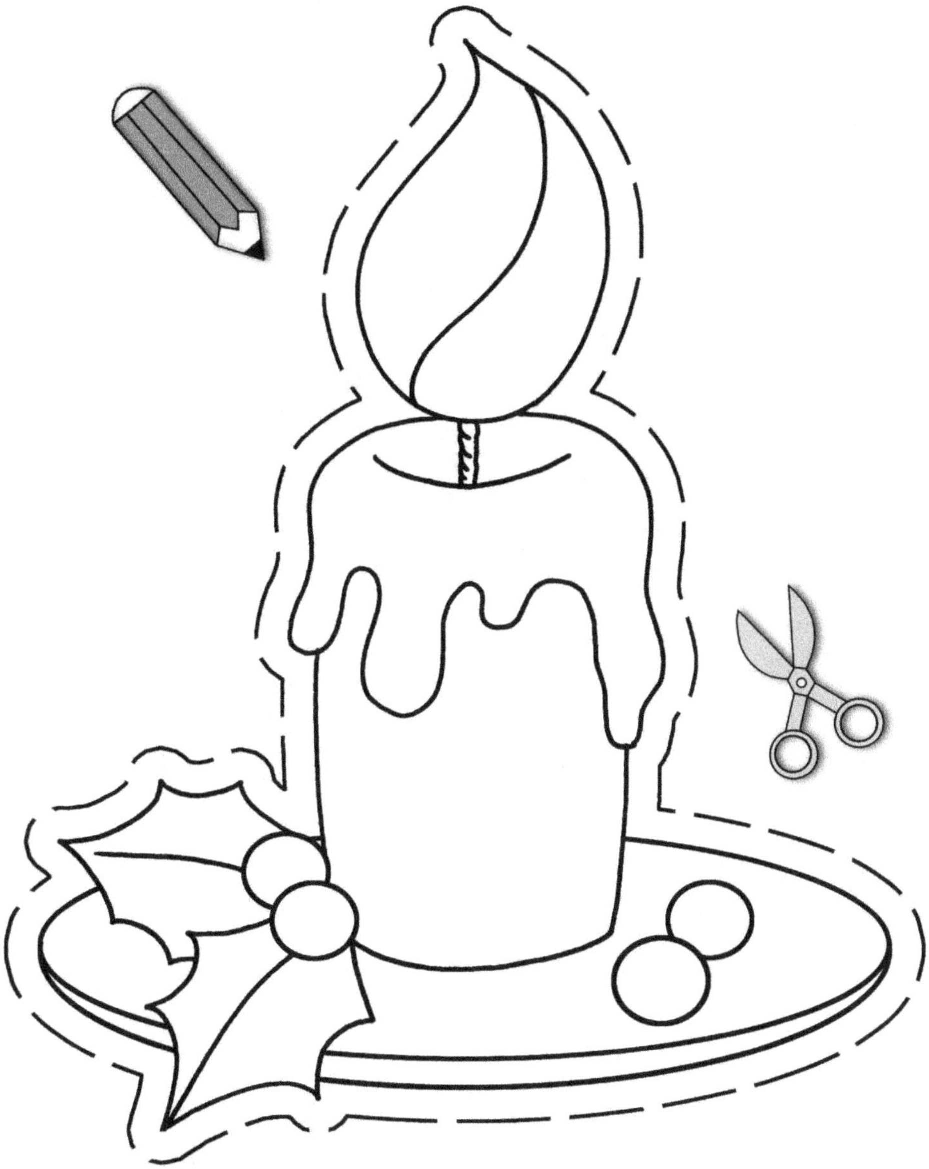

dot to dot

Connect the dots & color.

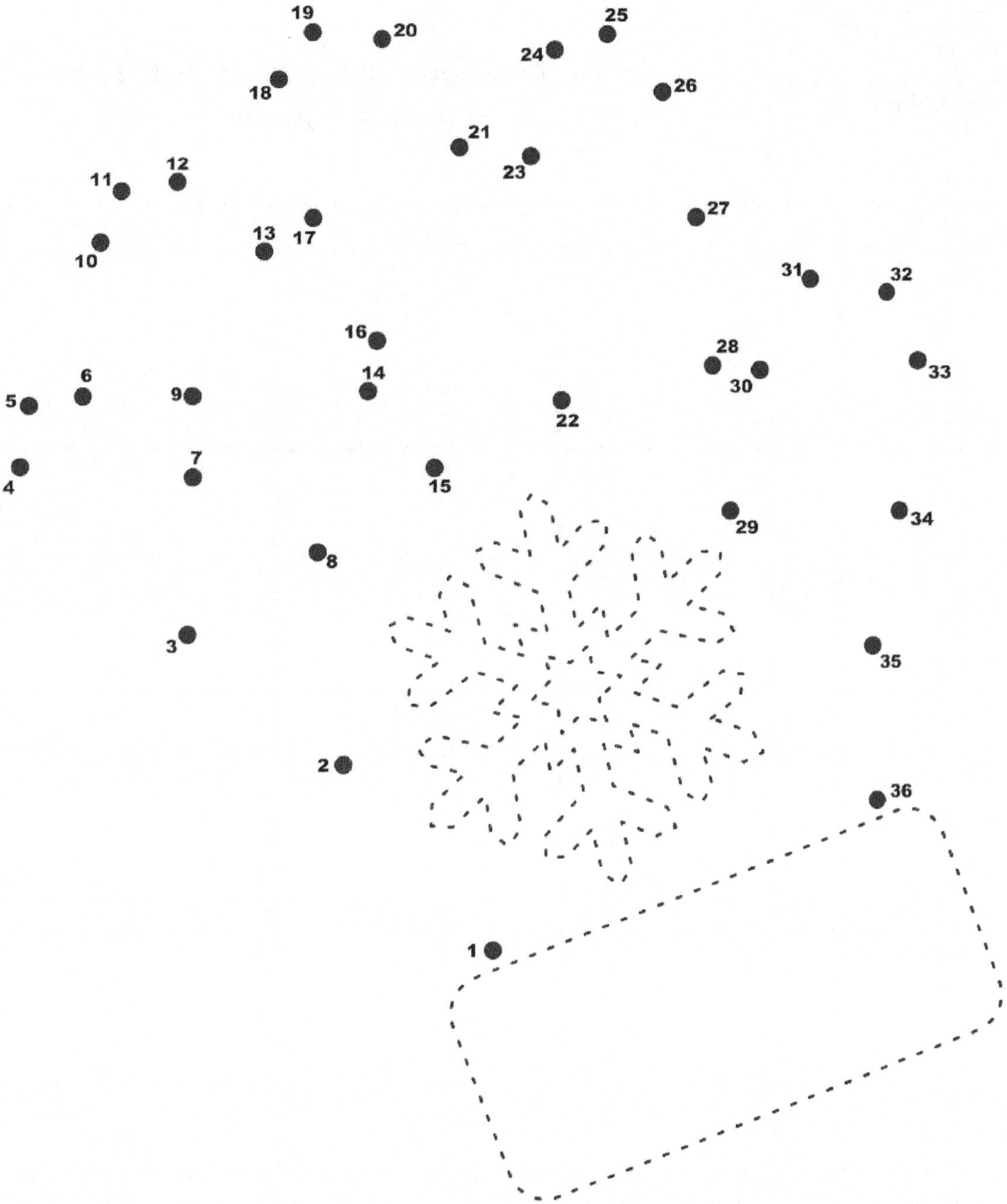

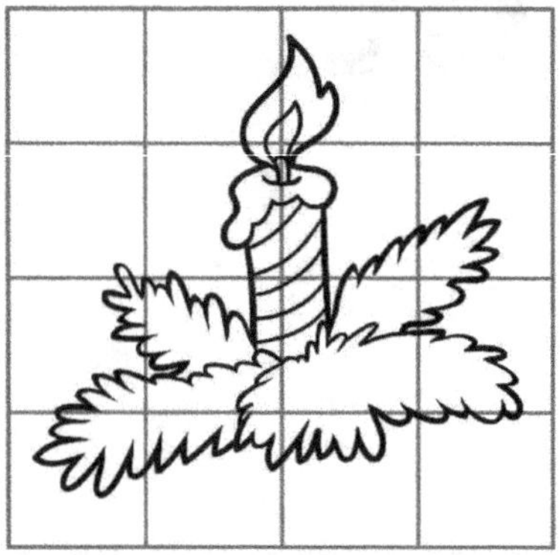

NETZANSCHLUSS

Verwende das Raster als Hilfslinie und zeichne das Bild

What do you see?

C___Y __N_

_T___I_G

W__A_H

HOW MANY CANDY CANES CAN YOU COUNT?

Match each Santa to his shadow

FILL THE SQUARES ON THE TREE

1. Ball 2. Lizard 3. Doll 4. Lollipop
5. Plane 6. Ship 7. Pencils 8. Skate
9. Sheep 10. Pirate 11. Elephant

COLOR & CUT

Color the image. Carefully cut with a scissors.
Make a hole and run a string through. Hang on the Christmas tree.

MATCH NUMBERS & ALPHABETS

connect the boys to their presents

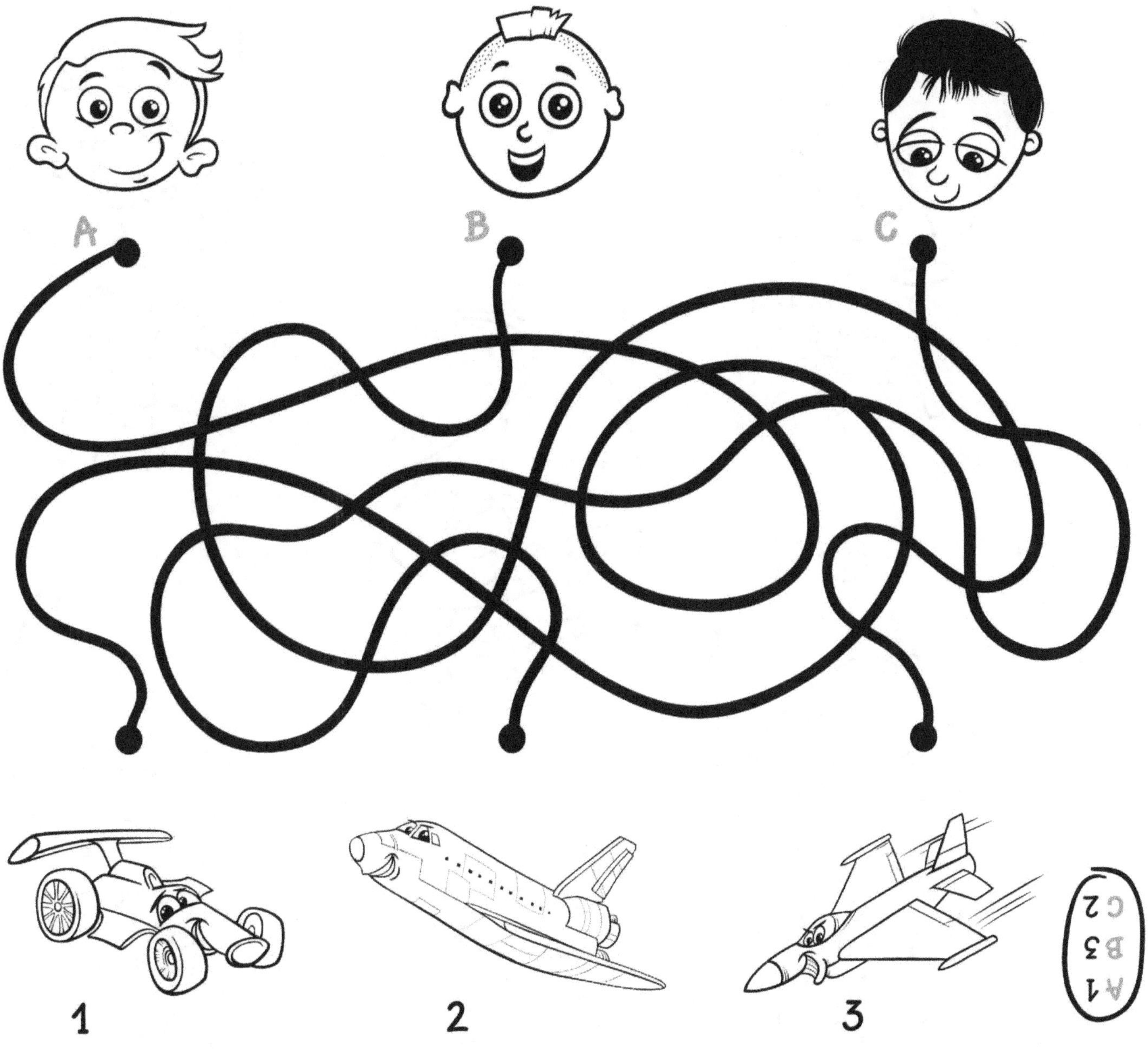

Santa's Helpers

How many Elves can you count?

COLOR ME!

GRID DRAW

Using the grid as a guide.
Copy the image

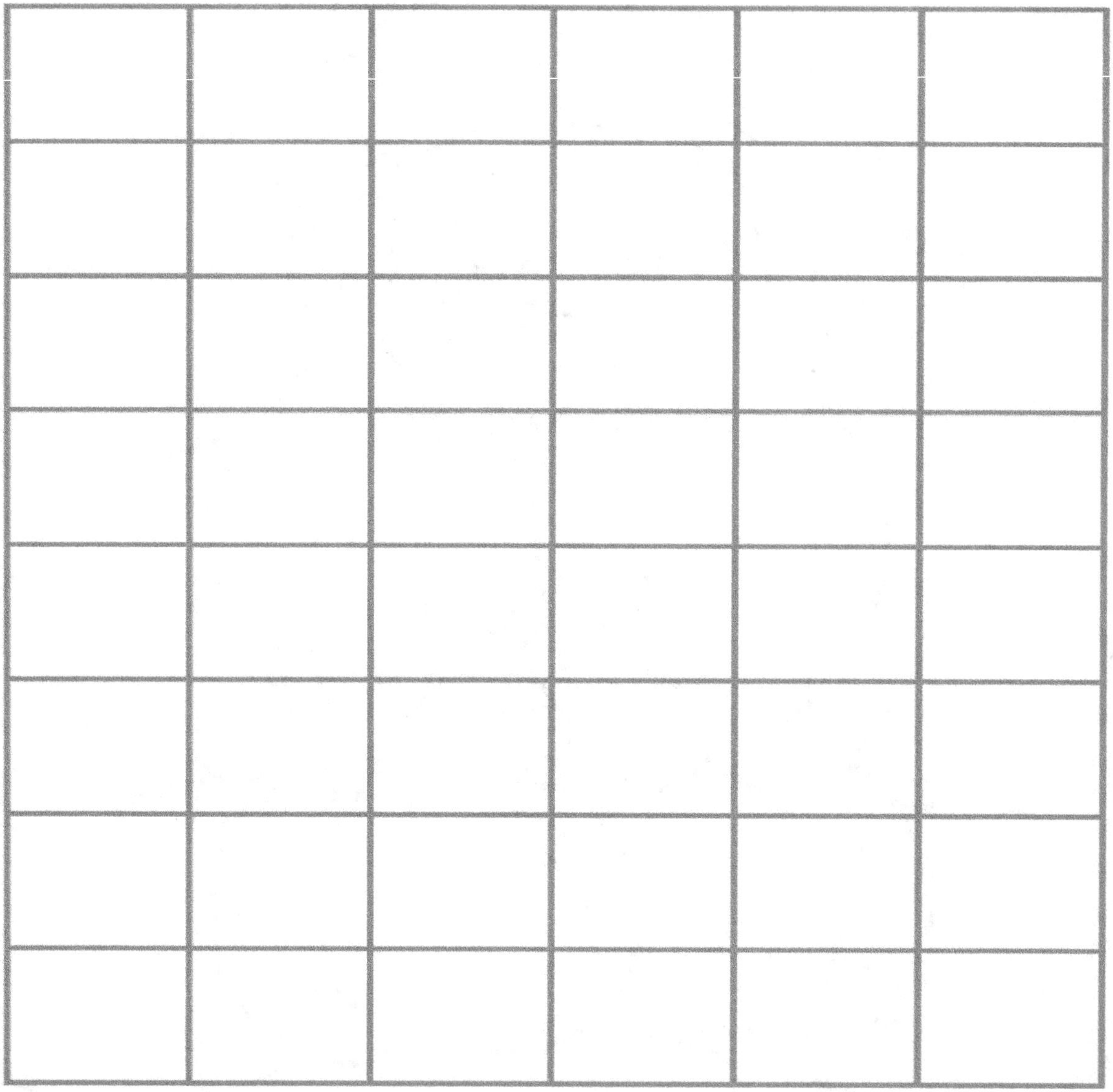

dot to dot

Connect the dots & color.

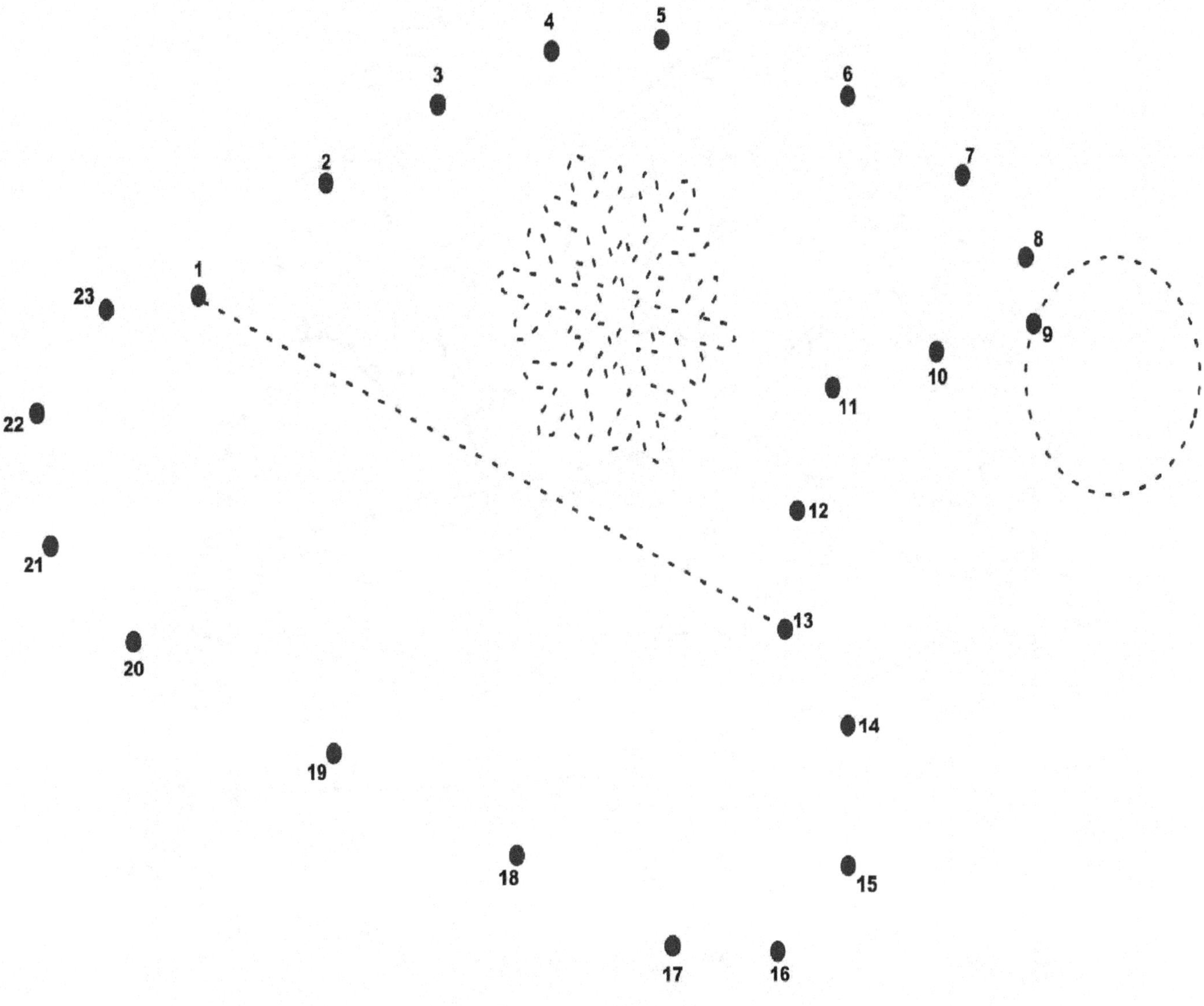

Color, Cut, Match & Paste

Color the Santa's outside the square.

Cut out each with a scissors.

Match and paste.

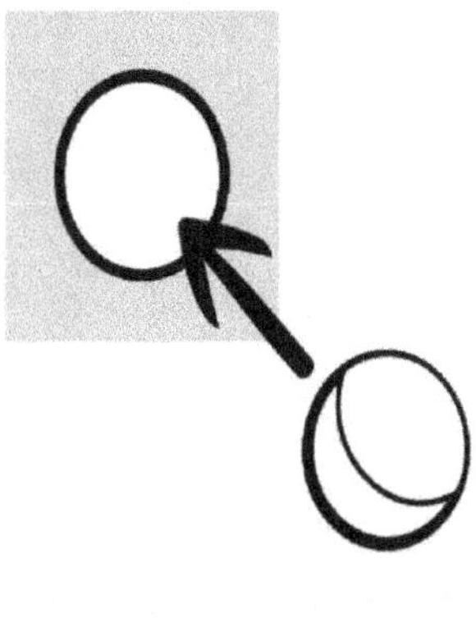

FILL THE SQUARES ON THE TREE

1. Unicorn 2. Sheep 3. Elf 4. Dress 5. Robot
6. Berry 7. Plane 8. Watch 9. Gorilla 10. Scooter
11. Santa 12. Celebration

Lost in the Maze

Help Mary get to her present

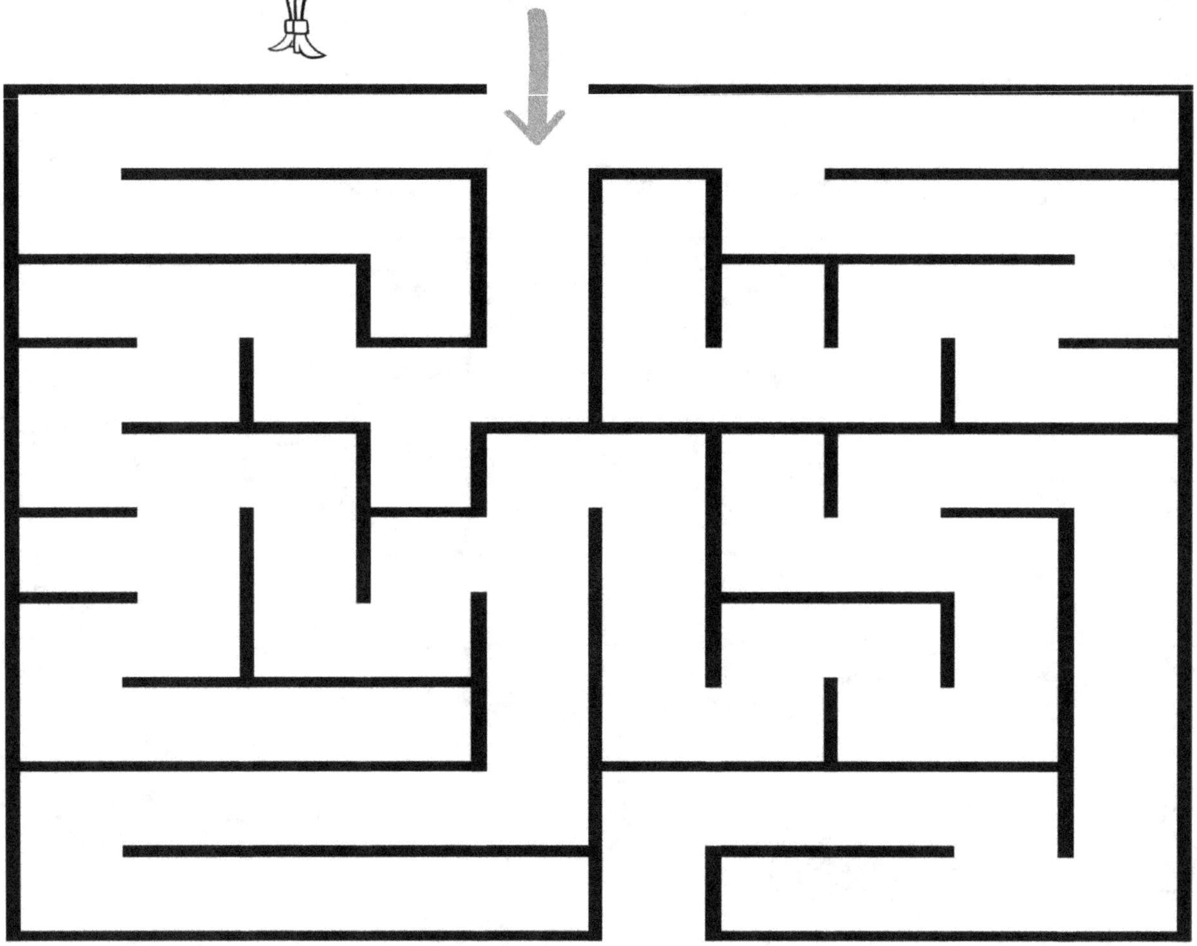

COLOR & CUT

Color the image. Carefully cut with a scissors.
Make a hole and run a string through. Hang on the Christmas tree.

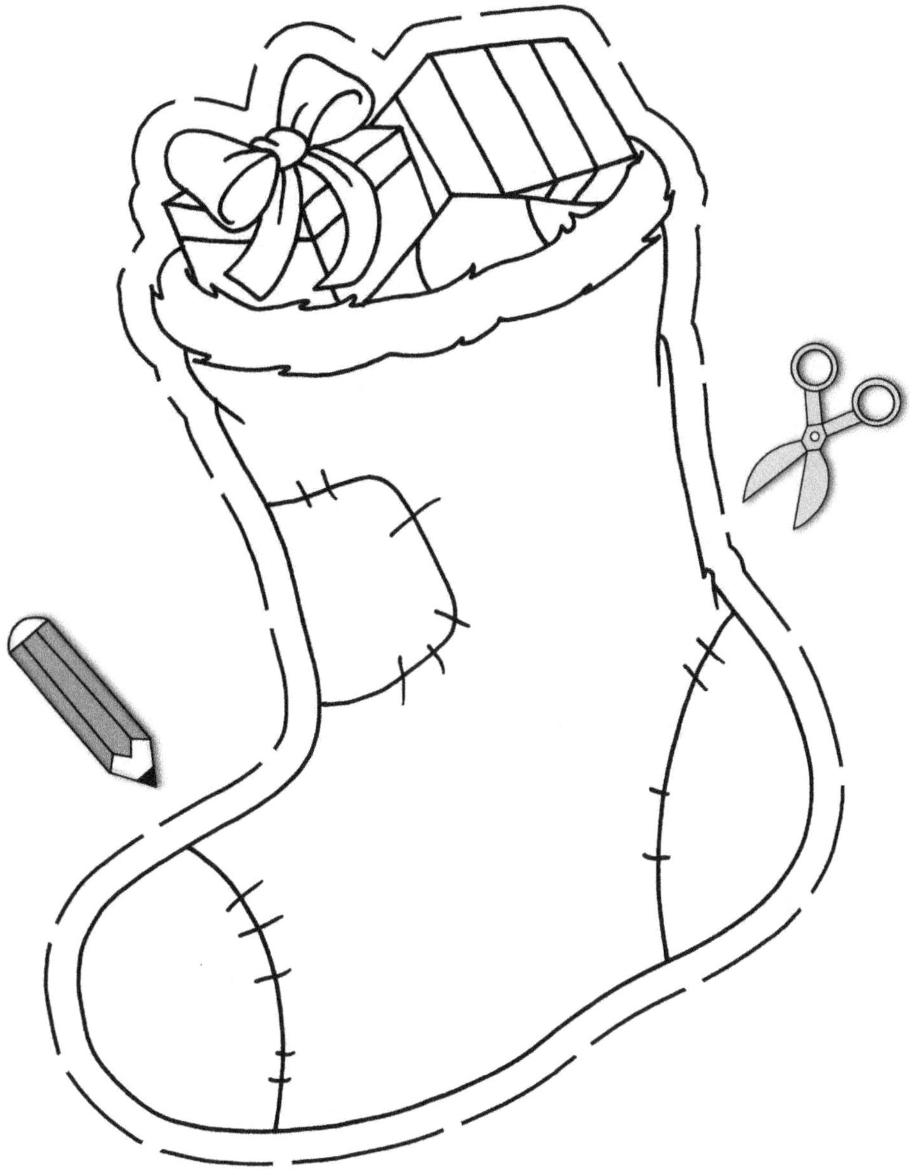

How many Christmas trees can you count?

dot to dot

Connect the dots & color.

What do you see?

Add the missing alphabets

_A_T_

_R___Y

C__IS_M_S T___

COLOR & CUT

Color the image. Carefully cut with a scissors.
Make a hole and run a string through. Hang on the Christmas tree.

GRID DRAW

Using the grid as a guide.
Copy the image

dot to dot

Connect the dot and color

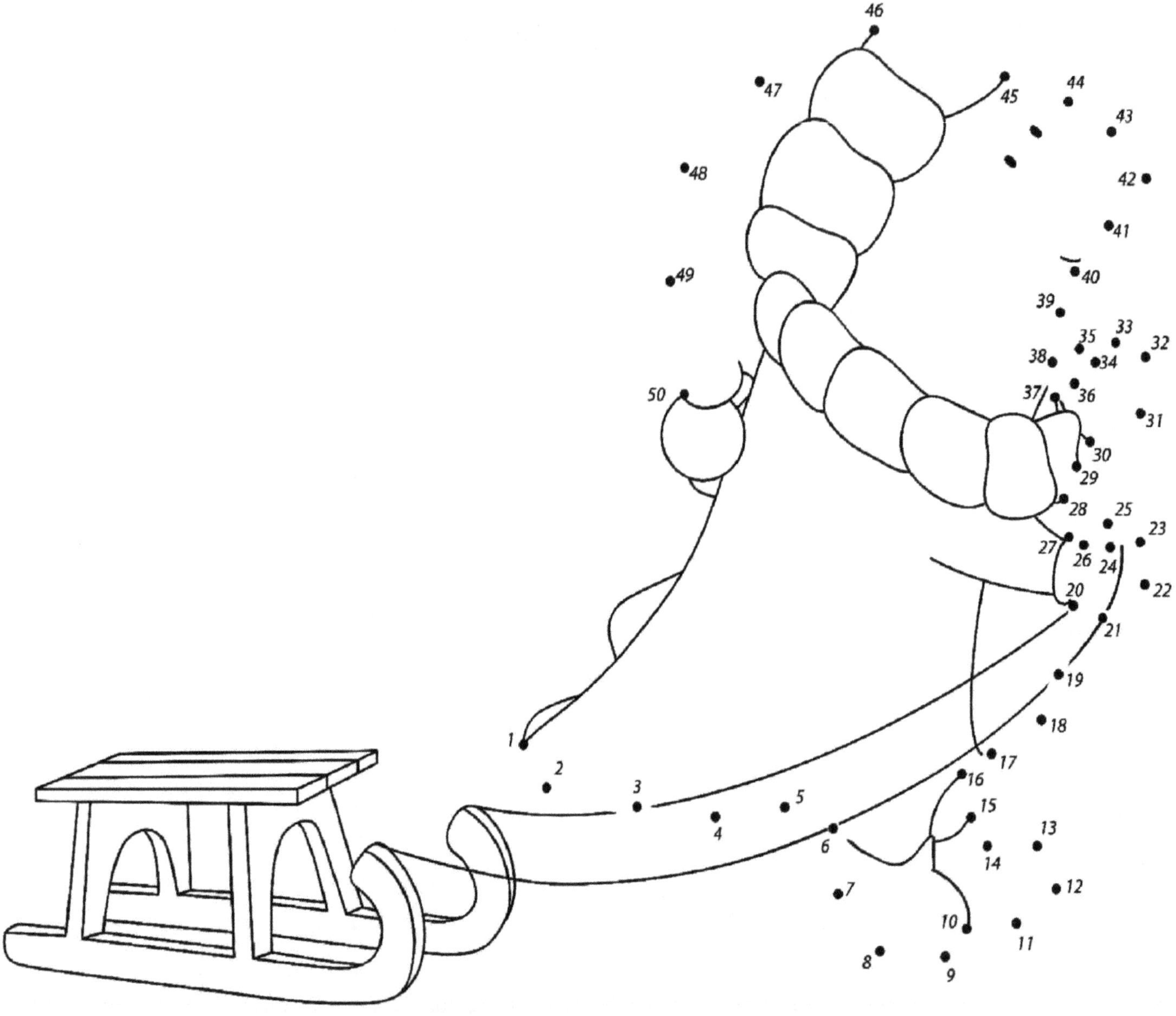

COLOR & CUT

Color the image and carefully cut using a scissors. Make a hole, add a string and hang on the Christmas tree.

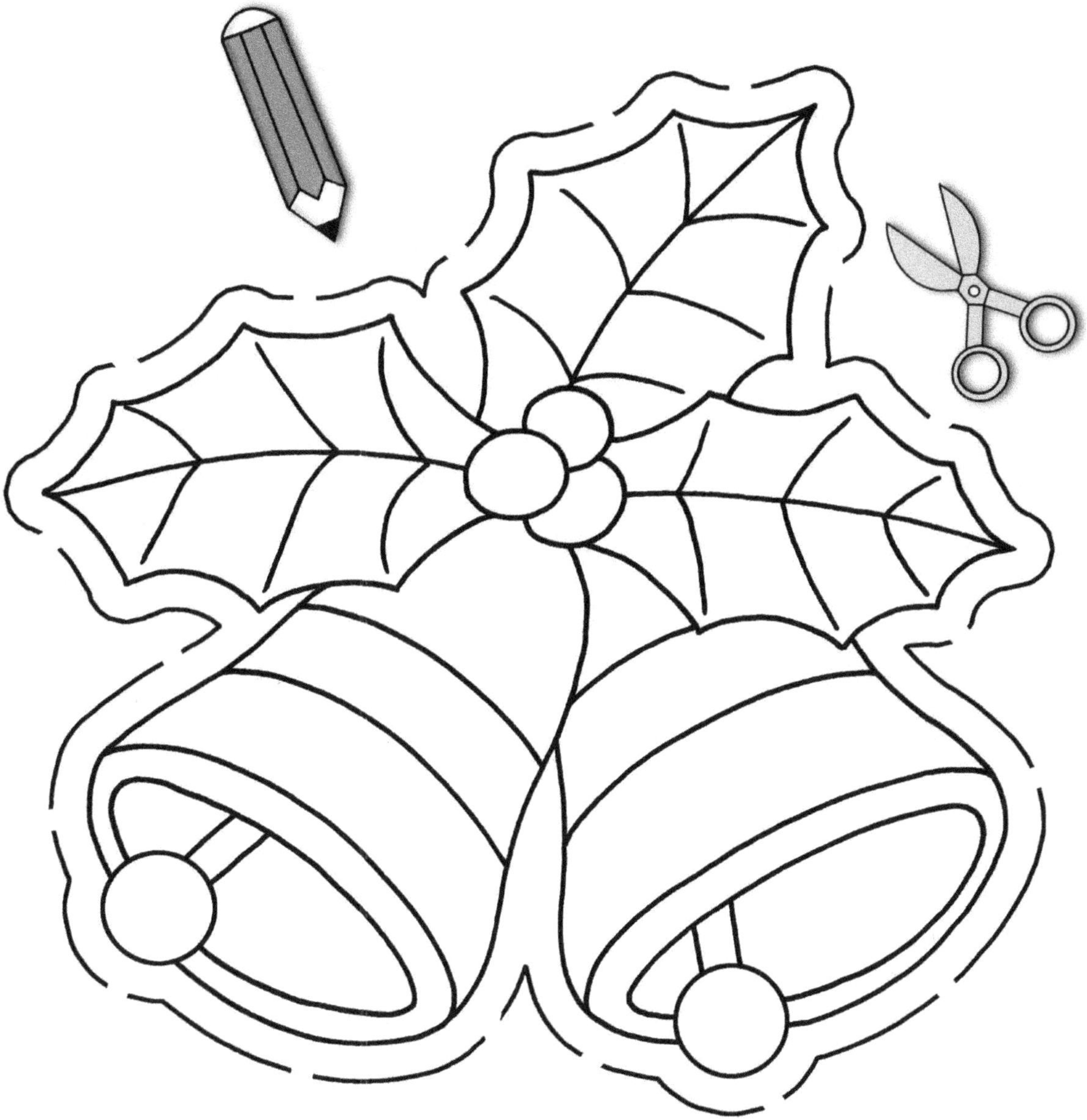

COLOR 2 SIMILAR WOOL HATS

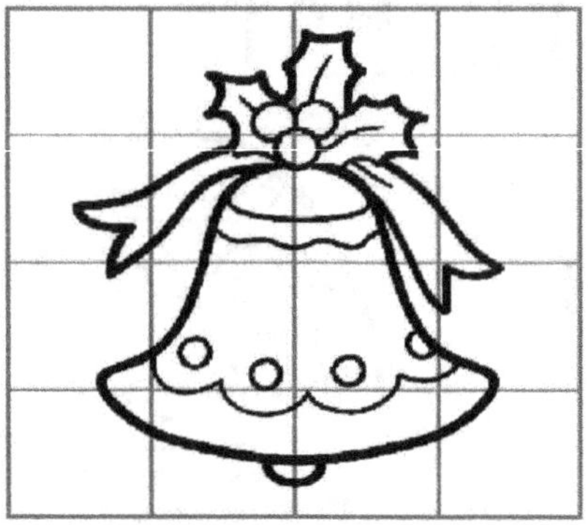

grid draw

Use the grid as a guide and draw the image

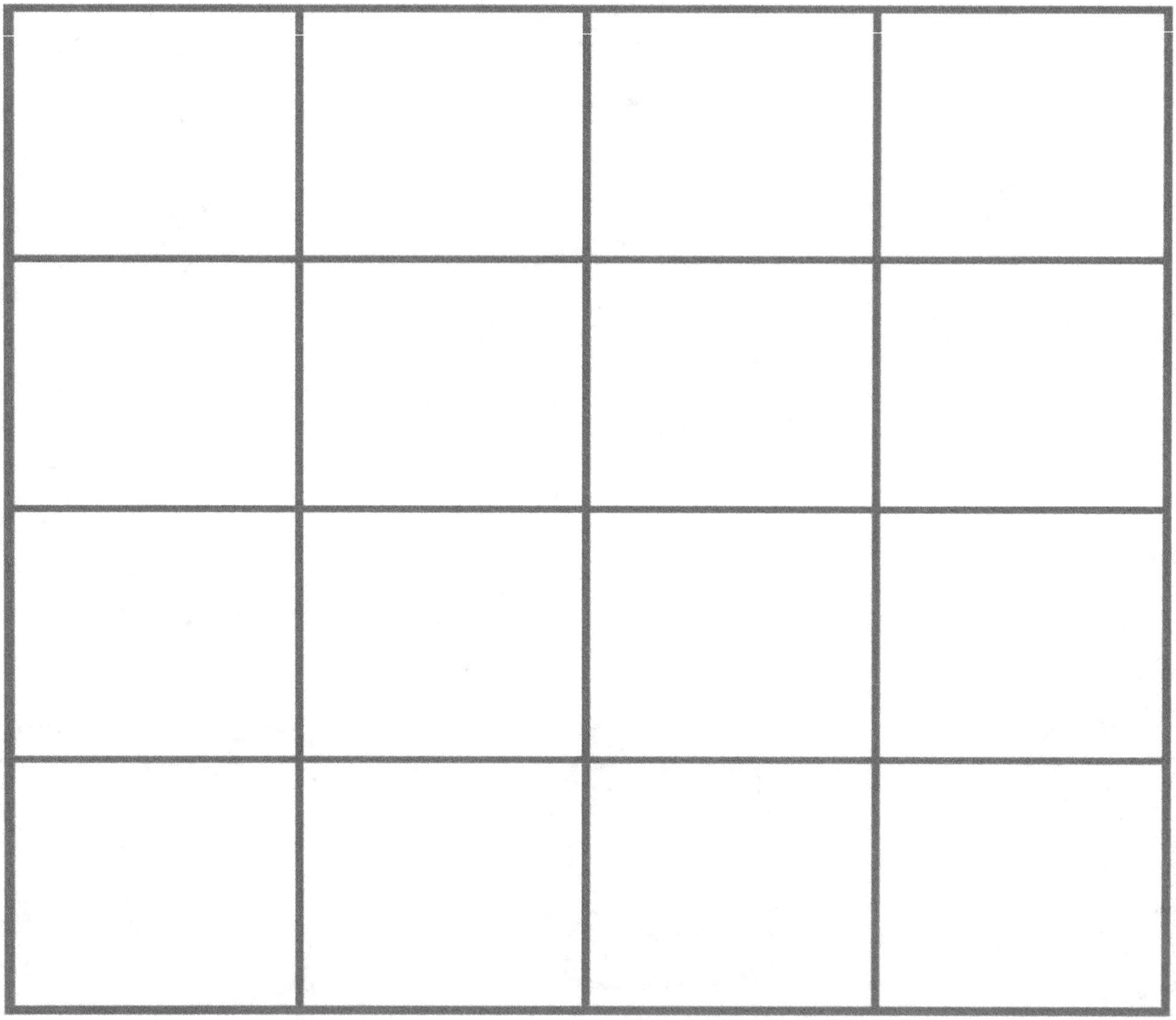

Color by numbers

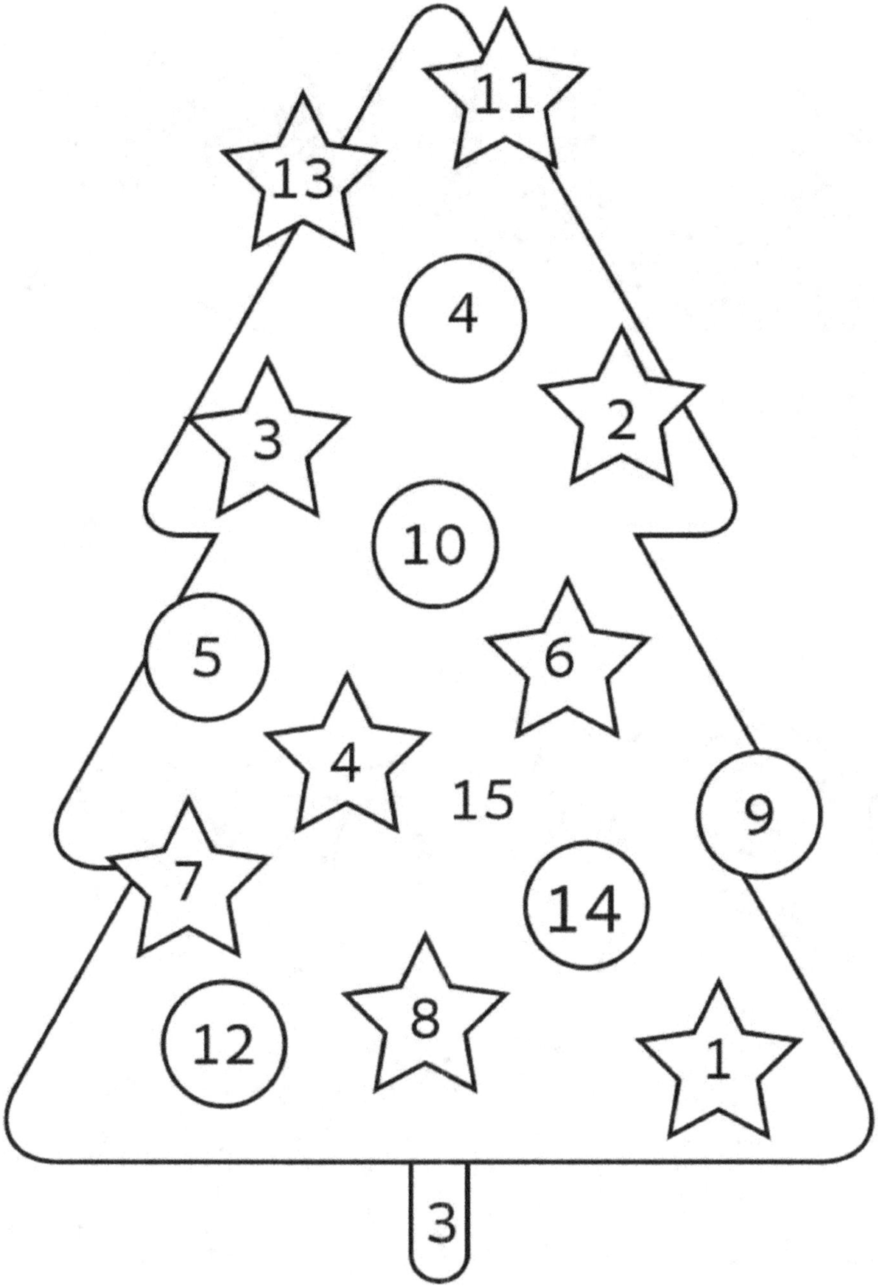

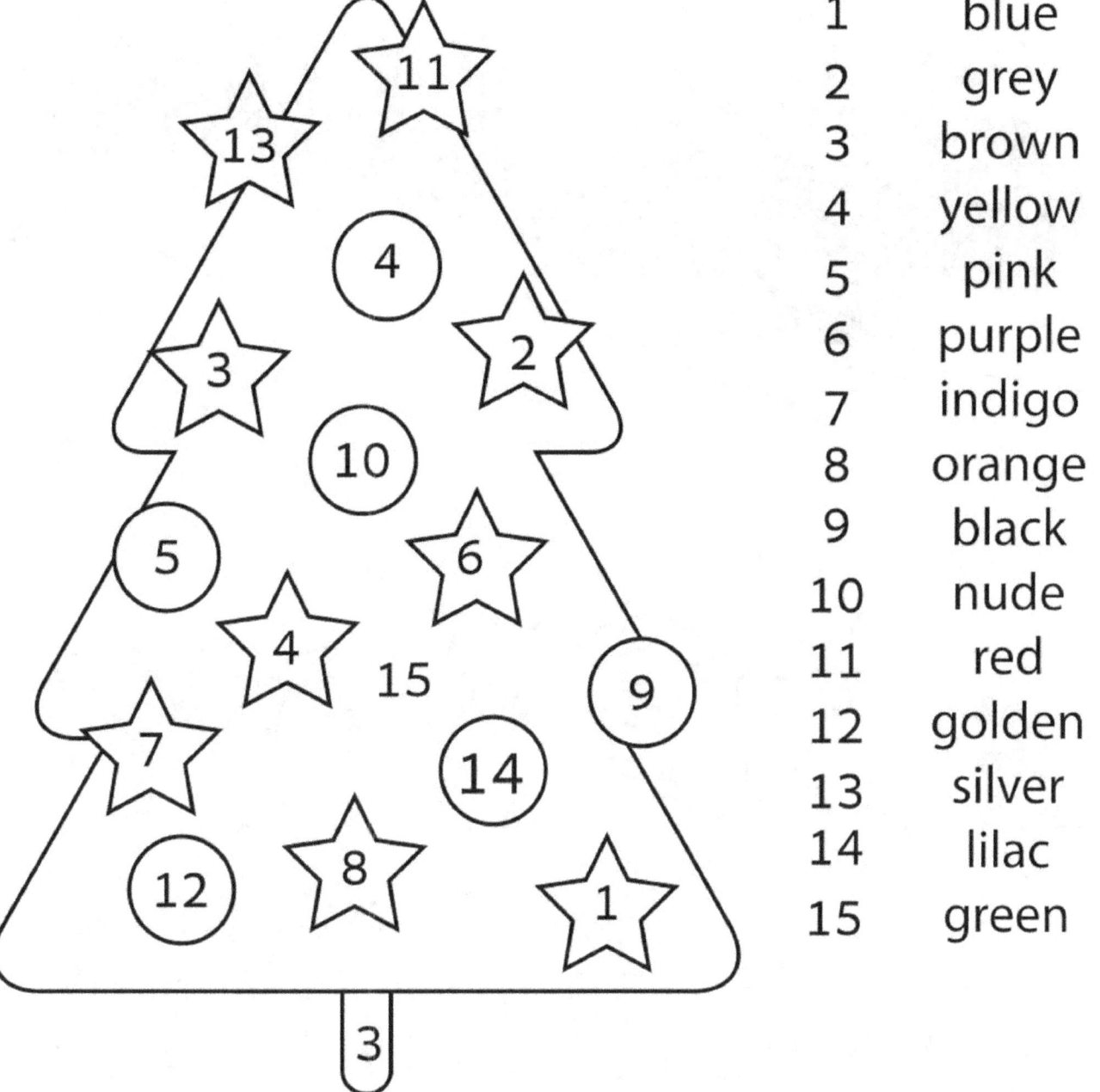

1	blue
2	grey
3	brown
4	yellow
5	pink
6	purple
7	indigo
8	orange
9	black
10	nude
11	red
12	golden
13	silver
14	lilac
15	green

MERRY
CHRISTMAS

NEW YEARS EVE!!

COLOR IN THE YEAR HERE!

Write your New Years Resolutions Here
New Years Resolutions
1.
2.
3.
4.

www.ingramcontent.com/pod-product-compliance
Lightning Source LLC
Chambersburg PA
CBHW081354080526
44588CB00016B/2500
9781945601323